SHAMELESS

HOW GOD'S GRACE ERASES OUR SHAME

PRESENTED TO

BY

DATE

Lifeway Press®
Brentwood, Tennessee

ISBN 978-1-4300-9510-1
Item 005847576
Dewey Decimal Classification Number: 242
Subject Heading: DEVOTIONAL LITERATURE / BIBLE STUDY AND TEACHING / GOD

Printed in the United States of America.

Student Ministry Publishing
Lifeway Resources
200 Powell Place, Suite 100
Brentwood, Tennessee 37027

We believe that the Bible has God for its author; salvation for its end; truth, without any mixture of error, for its matter; and that all Scripture is totally true and trustworthy. To review Lifeway's doctrinal guideline, please visit https://www.lifeway.com/about/doctrinal-guidelines.

---

publishing team

Director, NextGen Ministries
Chuck Peters

Manager, Small Group Resources
Karen Daniel

Writer
Ross Harvey

Content Editor
Kyle Wiltshire

Production Editor
April-Lyn Caouette

Graphic Designer
Shiloh Stufflebeam

Table of Contents

INTRO

I very clearly remember the first trip I took to Walt Disney World with my family when I was a child. One of the rides that stands out in my memory was the Grand Prix Raceway (which is called the Tomorrowland Speedway now). It's the first time I remember driving a car all by myself, and it was awesome.

A few years ago I took my own kids to Disney World for our first time there as a family. I told them about this cool ride I rode when I was a kid where you could actually drive a car—no matter how old you were! I was excited to relive my childhood memory with my own children.

But when we were buckled into the cars and they gave us the green light to go, a huge swell of disappointment came over me. It was nothing like I remembered! The cars weren't very fast, and sometimes you'd have to slow down even more because there was another car in front of you. Plus, the wheels were terribly misaligned. No matter which way I turned the steering wheel, I ran into the rails that kept the car on track. Needless to say, my kids weren't very impressed.

In many ways, we're all like those cars from the Tomorrowland Speedway. We have a misalignment in our lives that, if we were left to our own choices, would cause us to go crashing into things and cause major destruction. That misalignment in our lives is called sin, and the only way that we can be realigned is through the grace of God. That's what this devotional book is all about.

We so desperately need God's grace in our lives. Not only does His grace erase our sin and shame, it restores us to a right relationship with God and teaches us how to show grace to others who have wronged us. God's grace never disappoints!

GETTING STARTED

This devotional contains thirty days of content, broken down into sections. Each day is divided into three elements—**discover**, **delight**, and **display**—to help you grow in your faith.

DISCOVER

This section helps you examine the Bible in light of who God is and determine what it says about your identity in relationship to Him. Included here is the daily Bible reading and key verses, along with illustrations and commentary to guide you as you learn more about God's Word.

DELIGHT

In this section, you'll be challenged by questions and activities that help you see how God is alive and active in every detail of His Word and your life.

DISPLAY

Here's where you take action. This section calls you to apply what you've learned through each day.

Each day also includes a prayer activity at the conclusion of the devotion.

Throughout the devotional, you'll also find extra items to help you connect with the topic personally, such as Scripture memory verses and interactive articles.

SECTION 1

SIN

It might seem odd to start a book about grace with a section on sin. However, without sin, there would be no need for grace. To live beyond our shame, we need to understand sin clearly.

DAY 1

One Rule

READ GENESIS 3.

I will put hostility between you and the woman,
and between your offspring and her offspring.
He will strike your head,
and you will strike his heel.
— Genesis 3:15

DISCOVER

When God created everything we can see (and everything we can't see, too!) He said that His creation was good. But when He created us, He said that humanity was *very* good! Everything was made exactly as He designed it. Everything was perfect. And inside of that perfection, Adam and Eve had a job to do: they were to protect and take care of everything that God had created. He showed them exactly how to do that; all they had to do was follow His directions for how to live. And He permitted them to do anything—except eat from the tree in the middle of the garden of Eden, the tree of the Knowledge of Good and Evil. Only one thing was off limits.

But our enemy, Satan, had a plan to throw God's world into chaos. He took the form of a serpent and tempted Adam and Eve to disobey God's rule. And they did: they ate of the forbidden tree. When they disobeyed God's one rule, sin entered creation.

Now, sin has corrupted every aspect of creation. Sickness and decay are in the world. Death has become part of life. Sin broke humanity's relationship with God; what was very good now has been stained. Adam and Eve were banished from God's presence. In one moment—with one decision—it seemed like all had been lost. But even though everything changed with Adam and Eve's actions, God knew that one day, He would send Someone (Jesus) whose actions would set everything right again.

DELIGHT

In your own words, describe why is sin a big deal.

What has been the result of sin in your life? How does it feel when people sin against you?

DISPLAY

Sin is a huge problem. As we read in Genesis 3:15, sin always has a big impact, even if it's just one sin. That is because sin always begins in the heart before it becomes an action.

Grab a big clear bowl and fill it with water. Then add one drop of food coloring or water additive. Notice how the drop of color starts by only affecting a small area of water, but then it spreads to color the entire bowl!

Sin has that same effect on us. Sin always affects us, often in ways we don't immediately notice. One sin makes it easier to sin again in that same way. Sometimes we even sin in a different way to cover it up. Before we know it, sin has taken a mile when we only wanted to give it an inch. This is why we should take sin seriously, just as God does. Sin is dangerous.

Dear Lord, help me to take sin seriously, as You do. Show me Your heart and help me to understand the destruction that disobedience causes. Help me to believe the truth and stay away from sin. Amen.

DAY 2

Who's Bad?

READ ROMANS 3:9-26.

For all have sinned and fall short of the glory of God.
— Romans 3:23

DISCOVER

When we think of good and evil, we often imagine it as a battle between angels and demons. Something is reassuring about believing that this battle occurs on a spiritual plane instead of involving each one of us. However, it's not that simple, and it isn't that pleasant. The Bible teaches that we are *all* part of this battle—and we are on the wrong side. Sin is what makes us wicked; when we sin, we choose to do evil. In God's eyes, we are His opponents rather than His allies.

Contrary to popular belief, the Bible does not teach that some people are naturally good while others are naturally bad. Every person is born with a "sin nature," which is why we all sin. We live according to this nature, just as fish swim because they are fish. No one is exempt from sin—we all fall short of God's standard of goodness. Only God is perfect and good. We cannot compare ourselves to Him because we consistently make mistakes. We lie, cheat, steal, and hate. We are jealous, selfish, lustful, and prideful. Our thoughts and actions go against God's nature, making us His enemies.

It might be hard to see ourselves this way, but when we deny our sin, we reject our need for a Savior. Amazingly, even though we have all sinned, God promised that we would be rescued. It is a good thing that God is good even though we are not, because His ultimate act of goodness—sending Jesus to die in our place—rescued us from our sinful nature.

DELIGHT

Do you view yourself as a sinner? Why or why not?

Have you ever justified your sin by saying something like, "Well, I'm still a good person!"? Why is that a false statement?

DISPLAY

God's mark of perfection is like shooting an arrow and hitting the exact center every time. In terms of our obedience, we miss the mark. Maybe it's just a little to the left or a little to the right, but sometimes we aren't even close. We don't do as God would. What have you thought or done today that wasn't what God would have done? Probably at least a few things. We are far from who God is. But that's what makes the truth—that He loves us and wants a relationship with us despite our sin—so amazing. In the space below, draw a target. In the center of the target, write "Jesus." Then, spend some time thanking God that Jesus hit the mark for us.

Dear God, thank You for loving me no matter what. Help me to see my evil thoughts, actions, and desires for what they really are. Help me to recognize when I am in rebellion toward You, and help me to turn away from the things I do that You don't want me to do. I love You, God. Amen.

DAY 3

Like a Bear

READ GENESIS 4:1-16.

"If you do what is right, won't you be accepted?
But if you do not do what is right, sin is crouching at the door.
Its desire is for you, but you must rule over it."
— Genesis 4:7

DISCOVER

When I was climbing in the mountains of Colorado, I remember being chiefly concerned with fighting against the high altitude, rocky terrain, and potentially extreme weather. One thing I wasn't prepared for was bears! A friend offered me this piece of advice: If you see a bear, keep your eyes on it. Never turn your back on a bear. If you run, it will trigger the bear to chase after you. It will want to make you a tasty treat!

Sin has a deep impact on everything around us. Every broken thing we see is a result of sin, but even more dangerously, sin is within us. If we aren't careful, it will quickly take over. Cain, Adam and Eve's firstborn son, was corrupted by sin. Although God warned him, he allowed sin to take over his thoughts and actions, which led him to murder his brother.

Sin seeks to distract us so that it can attack us, just like a bear. Sin doesn't want us to know that it's working against us at all times. It lurks and waits to pounce. Therefore, we must pay attention to the warning signs that sin is present and do everything we can to resist it. If we don't, it will consume us. Alone, we are powerless against sin and cannot overcome it.

DELIGHT

In your life, how has one sin led to more sin? How did you stop it?

What are some warning signs of sin in your heart?

DISPLAY

You can find videos of predators in the wild on TV or streaming services. The next time you are looking for something to watch, find a nature show that involves predators like bears or lions. Because of our enemy Satan, sin is like those predators. It wants to sneak up on you and take over your life. But there are warning signs of the dangers of sin. Like He did for Cain, God will help you to know when you are under attack. It's up to you to listen for His warnings.

God, thank You for not leaving us to be devoured by sin. Thank You for caring about us enough to warn us when we are walking the wrong way. Help me to be more sensitive to Your leading and to pay attention to Your guidance. Amen.

DAY 4

A Deadly Process

READ JAMES 1:13-15.

But each person is tempted when he is drawn away and enticed by his own evil desire. Then after desire has conceived, it gives birth to sin, and when sin is fully grown, it gives birth to death.
— James 1:14-15

DISCOVER

Have you ever seen how a fruit grows? An apple, watermelon, or banana doesn't begin that way. It starts as a seed, and then with the proper water, sunlight, and nourishment, it grows into a plant. When the plant is healthy and fully grown, it produces fruit. Something small grows into something much, much bigger.

A sinful thought or action doesn't come out of nowhere. It always starts small, with a temptation. A temptation is a desire to do something that we know goes against God's design. It's the pull we feel to sin. Temptation by itself isn't wrong—everyone has temptation in their lives. Even Jesus did (see Matt. 4:1-11).

When we are tempted, we still have time to squash the temptation before it becomes sin. But if we let it grow, we won't be able to contain it—and unchecked sin leads to death. And if we don't have faith in Jesus, that means separation from God forever. But sin is deadly even for the believer. Sin in our lives kills relationships, opportunities, friendships, and the peace that God wants for us. We should be quick to stop temptation while it is just a seed, before it grows into something dangerous.

DELIGHT

Where does sin usually begin in your life? What most often leads you to fall into temptation?

Read James 4:7. How can you resist temptation? What action steps do you need to take to stay away from its pull?

DISPLAY

Make a list of your biggest temptations. Sometimes naming your weak points and seeing them on paper will alert you to where, who, or what you need to avoid. Ask a trusted friend for accountability in these weak spots, and pray for strength to fight against temptation.

God, thank You for giving me time to defeat temptation before it turns into sin. Help me to resist temptation. Help me to pull away from sin and continually turn to You for deliverance. And thank You for Your Word, which guides us in our lives. Amen.

DAY 5

Let's Do Good

READ JAMES 4.

So it is sin to know the good and yet not do it.
— James 4:17

DISCOVER

Have you ever found yourself in a situation where you knew the right thing to do, but you chose not to do anything? It could be forgiving someone who has hurt you or befriending someone you've been avoiding. Sometimes, it's as simple as cleaning your room because your mom asked you to. We usually think of sin as doing something we shouldn't do, but sometimes, it can also be not doing something we should do.

God's Word tells us not only what we shouldn't do, but also what we should do. He wants us to live a life that pleases Him by serving others and treating people with kindness and compassion. When we deliberately choose not to do what we know is right, we are sinning.

God wants us to be part of the solution to the brokenness in this world. By doing good in His name, we can partially reverse the destructive effects of sin. However, when we know what is good and fail to act on it, we become part of the problem, allowing the effects of sin to continue. When we have the opportunity and resources to do good, we must act on it. Failing to do so goes against God's plan and purpose for us.

DELIGHT

What is something good you knew you should do but didn't?

Why does it go against God's design when we act wrongly?

Why does it go against God's design when we fail to act rightly even when we know what we should do?

DISPLAY

One right thing you can make a habit of doing is providing for the homeless in your community. Make a homeless bag: take a large resealable bag and pack it with toiletry items, socks, water bottles, wet wipes, and other items. Keep them in your car or your parent's car for the next time you see someone in need. Make a practice of acting when you can do good.

Dear Lord, help me to obey Your leading when You want me to help heal the brokenness of this world. Allow me to be someone who changes the world for the better. Help me to spread Your love to others. Amen.

DAY 6

Inside vs Outside

READ MARK 7:1-23.

"For from within, out of people's hearts, come evil thoughts, sexual immoralities, thefts, murders, adulteries, greed, evil actions, deceit, self-indulgence, envy, slander, pride, and foolishness."
— Mark 7:21-22

DISCOVER

My son loves fruit. Whenever it's summertime, he especially enjoys watermelon. If we let him, he would eat an entire one by himself! Watermelon is tricky to buy, though. It is hard to know from the outside if the watermelon is good on the inside. You can see the external features, but the inside is what is important.

Jesus often clashed with the Jewish religious leaders of His time, the Pharisees. They were a lot like a bad watermelon: they prioritized looking good on the outside, but their inside was rotten.

We must be careful not to live in the same way. Sin is a big deal and our outsides don't always show what's going on in our hearts and minds. We make sure that what others can see—like what we look like and the surface-level areas of obedience—looks right. But Jesus says we should take a careful look at what's inside, instead. From deep within come destructive patterns and evil thoughts. Jesus is most concerned with what is inside of us because when sin is in our hearts, it can be easy to hide. Hidden, internal sin is the most dangerous.

DELIGHT

When are you most tempted to act like you are all good while on the inside you are struggling?

Why is it dangerous to put up this type of illusion?

Why is it dangerous to ignore sin and hide it from yourself?

DISPLAY

Read Psalm 119:11. One way to help sin out of your heart is by hiding God's Word inside of it. Memorize Psalm 119:11, and plan to memorize more of God's Word as you continue this devotional. Keeping your heart full of truth will help you examine deep within and keep you aligned to God's desires.

Dear God, help me to see what is truly in my heart. I want to make sure that sin doesn't hide within me and that my desires are what You want. Help me to listen to You and to others who know me well. Thank You for caring about my heart. Amen.

Memory Verse

Psalm 119:11

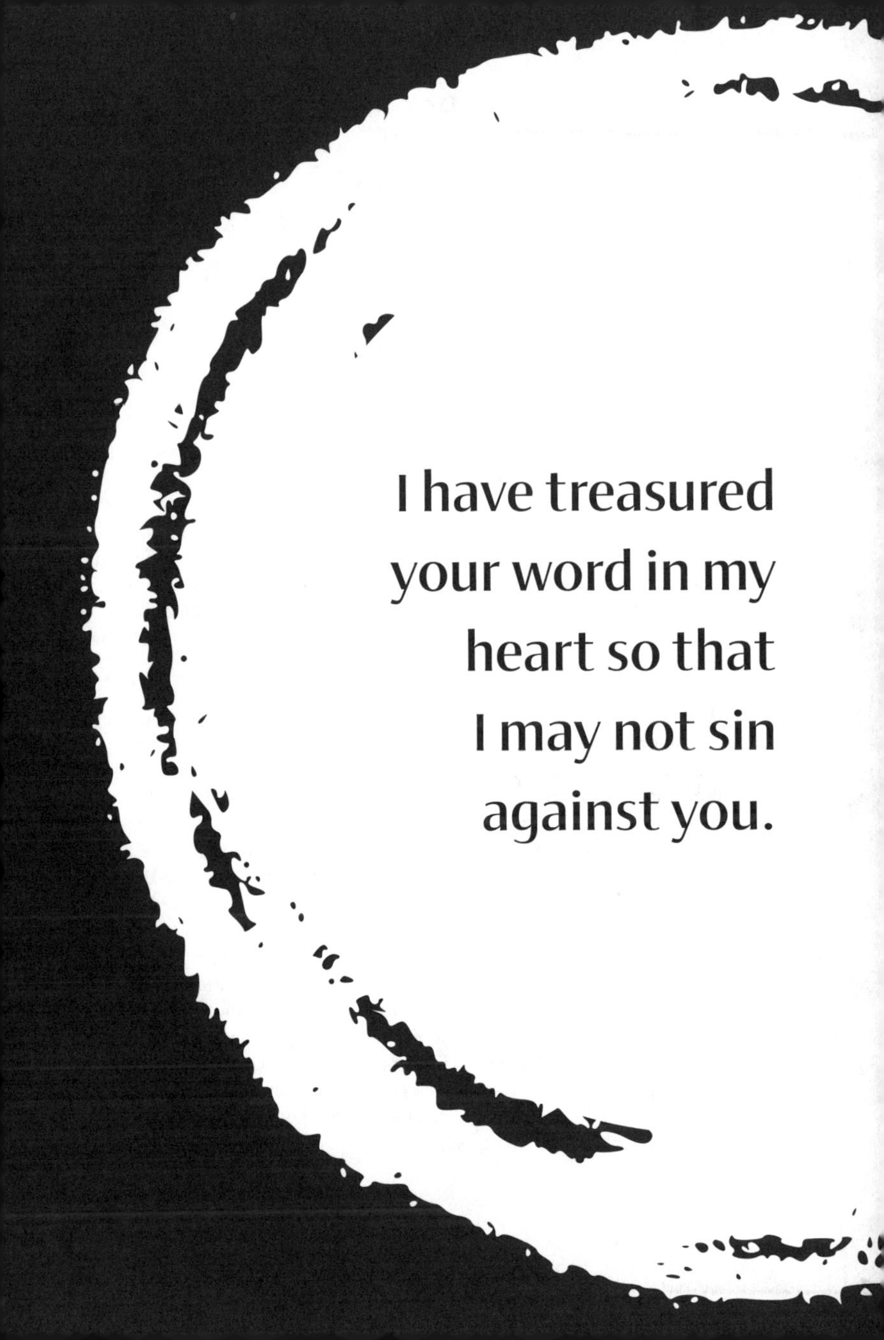
I have treasured
your word in my
heart so that
I may not sin
against you.

DAY 7

Like a Lion

READ 1 JOHN 3:1-10.

Everyone who commits sin practices lawlessness; and sin is lawlessness.
— 1 John 3:4

DISCOVER

I once saw a video of a man who kept taunting a lion. He would swat at it and provoke it, believing that he could escape to safety before the lion became angry and attacked him. He would hop away when the lion got close. But, one time he got too close—and the lion got a nibble of his arm. At that point, he probably learned his lesson that a lion was nothing to be played with.

Sin is powerful, too. It seeks to keep us bound and ignorant of the truth. Jesus is the only one who can free us from the chains of sin and death. However, even after we have a relationship with Jesus, we will continue to face temptation and struggle against sin, because we are still affected by it. Our sinful nature will often pull us to do things that we know are wrong. When we do sin, the Holy Spirit will remind us of the truth and invite us to repent and return to God. He warns us against falling back into that old pattern.

As followers of Jesus, we cannot continue to practice sin. Doing so goes against the new nature that Jesus gives us and contradicts the gospel (see 2 Cor. 5:17). Although we may struggle with sin, we should never allow it to control our lives. If we find ourselves living in sin without repentance or guidance from God, it's important to talk to a trusted adult or pastor. A pattern of unrepentant sin is dangerous and is evidence of a lack of a relationship with God. Christians should not be comfortable continually provoking the lion of sin.

DELIGHT

Be honest with yourself: What is a sin or temptation in your life that you consistently struggle with? How can you offer this sin or temptation to God?

When you struggle, how does the Holy Spirit guide you?

DISPLAY

Read John 14:12-28. Jesus promised that the Holy Spirit would come to live inside believers to help them in their lives. One of the things the Holy Spirit does is remind believers of what Jesus says. He reminds us of what is true. When we sin, the Holy Spirit reminds us that God's way is better. If you don't feel the Holy Spirit convicting you when you sin, confide in someone at your church (or another trusted adult) to continue this conversation and discover what steps you need to take.

Dear God, thank You for giving me the Holy Spirit to lead me away from sin. Help me to listen to Him when He speaks to me. Please help me not entertain sin in my life; help me to take it seriously. I love You, God. Amen.

DAY 8

We Are Who We Are

READ GALATIANS 5:16-26.

I am warning you about these things — as I warned you before — that those who practice such things will not inherit the kingdom of God.
— Galatians 5:21

DISCOVER

If you saw a pink, curly-tailed animal rolling around in the mud, what would you say that it was? Hopefully, you would say that it is a pig. You can tell what things are by the way they act. A pig acts like a pig because it is a pig. Rolling in mud is in its nature and character. A car drives on the road and runs on gasoline because it is a car. And so on.

In Galatians 5, Paul teaches about the works of the flesh—sinful things—versus the works of the Holy Spirit. Every person is born with a tendency toward sinfulness, so everyone naturally lives in sin and commits works of the flesh. Once you have a relationship with God through faith and trust in Jesus as Savior and Lord, you receive the Holy Spirit. He produces the works of the Spirit through you because a believer is a new creation led by the Spirit, not the flesh.

This is why Paul warns the believer not to continue to produce "fleshly" works. It is not who you are anymore. Those who continually produce works of the flesh and not works of the Spirit will not inherit the kingdom of God because they do not have a relationship with Jesus. Followers of Jesus act like Jesus because of who is in them: the Holy Spirit. We cannot live according to the flesh anymore, because it isn't our nature and character any longer.

DELIGHT

Where are you currently living outside of your nature as a believer?

What are you doing to return to God's design for you?

Read 2 Corinthians 5:17. What does Paul say about the believer?

DISPLAY

Search for 2 Corinthians 5:17 on your phone and take a screenshot of it. Set it as your phone's background. Use this truth to remind you of who you are. If you are in Christ, you are made new in Him. Therefore, the believer cannot continue to produce works of sin.

Dear God, help me to believe that I am not my sin. Thank You for making me a new creation in Christ. Help me to not fear sin but to know that You are more powerful than it. Amen.

DAY 9

Hide and Seek

READ PROVERBS 28:13.

The one who conceals his sins
will not prosper,
but whoever confesses and renounces them
will find mercy.

DISCOVER

Someone once spilled coffee on the gray rug in our living room. Since the spill was near the couch, I could have just moved the rug over a few inches so that the spill was hidden. But that wouldn't have solved the issue. Instead, I brought the spill into view, applied warm water and carpet cleaner, and washed the stain out.

Often when we make a mistake, we try to cover it up. Just as it was for Adam and Eve in Genesis 3, shame is normally the first emotion we feel. Because of this shame, we try to hide our mistakes. We try to cover up our sin. Psychologists say hiding our mistakes is damaging to our emotional and physical health and even increases our shame. It is no surprise that God, who designed and created us, says the same thing and even gives us the remedy.

In Proverbs 28, we are warned against hiding our sins. We often try to hide them from ourselves, from others, and from God. Satan wants us to feel alone, and that's what happens when we keep our sins to ourselves. However, the key to freedom is quite the opposite. God promises us His mercy if we confess our sins and turn away from them. We should be quick to admit our sins, tell God about them, and even confess them to close and trusted friends. We need to bring our sins to light and let God apply His mercy—it's the only way our sins can be cleansed and removed from us.

DELIGHT

When was a time you tried to cover up your sin instead of confessing it to God?

How do you feel when you conceal your sin? Better or worse? Why?

DISPLAY

Do you know what the last sin you committed was? Make a practice of confessing and repenting from your sin. Start by telling God about what you did. Then, tell a trusted friend. Actively confessing and repenting from your sin will help you fight against shame and make it easier to continue to bring your sin to the light.

Dear God, thank You for being willing to give mercy to me. Help me not to be ashamed of my sin, and help me to bring it to You instead. Please put people in my life who will help me to fight against sin and be honest. Thank You for every good gift You give, including Your patience and mercy. Amen.

DAY 10

A Just Judge

READ HEBREWS 10:26-31.

It is a terrifying thing to fall into the hands of the living God.
— Hebrews 10:31

DISCOVER

A fair judge will deliver the appropriate justice to those he or she deems guilty, even if that judge doesn't personally want to. Let's say the judge's son or daughter is the one who commits the crime. If the judge is just, he or she will still give an appropriate sentence (punishment). The law must come first. The judge's job is to uphold the law because the order and design of society depend on it.

Sin is a serious thing. God loves us, but His perfect rules say that anyone who sins deserves to be separated from Him. Since God Himself is love and life, anyone who sins receives spiritual death. Those who do not turn away from their sin and accept Jesus's sacrifice in their place will be separated from God forever when they die.

God loves us and wants a relationship with us, but He cannot change His law. The truth is that sin will be punished: either we will be judged for our sin or we accept that Jesus was judged for us and we place our faith in Him. There is no other option.

DELIGHT

What would the world be like if God didn't have rules?

Why are God's rules actually a great thing for us?

DISPLAY

On a sheet of paper, write down some rules that are in the world today. On the other side of the paper, write down the reasoning behind those rules. Underneath each rule, write down the punishment for breaking it. In God's perfect design, He has given us the wisdom to make rules and to give out appropriate judgment for breaking them. But God's rules and punishments are perfect. We must trust them, even when we don't fully understand everything He does.

Dear God, help me to trust You more even when I don't understand. Help me to follow Your rules and love Your laws. Thank You that I do not have to spend eternity away from You. Thank You for sending Jesus to make a way back to You. Amen.

SECTION 2

GRACE

In Section 1, we learned about sin. But did you notice that just about all the verses you read about sin also talked about forgiveness, mercy, and grace? God loves to and longs to show us grace and erase our shame.

DAY 11

Undeserved Favor

READ ROMANS 5:1-11.

But God proves his own love for us in that while we were still sinners, Christ died for us.
— Romans 5:8

DISCOVER

Imagine that you let a friend borrow five bucks, but when you asked for the money back, your friend couldn't pay it. No big deal, right? You have five dollars less, but that's not a big problem. Now, imagine a friend borrows fifty thousand dollars! You're definitely going to expect that to be repaid. But would you ever, under any circumstances, loan your enemy any money? Probably not, and you certainly wouldn't give an enemy an amount that large!

The incredible thing about what Jesus did for us is that He didn't pay a sum of money for our salvation—He gave up His own life. In Romans 5, Paul reminds us that Jesus died for us while we were still sinners, His enemies. We owed a debt that we could never pay, and the consequences of our sins meant death.

Like someone who is dead, we couldn't change our fate on our own. Only someone who had a record of perfection and the power to give life could volunteer to take our sins upon Himself. Jesus did that, and we could never repay Him for it. He was willing to save us simply because of His grace and love, not because we deserved it. And that's what grace is: undeserved favor. Jesus dying in our place is the greatest gift the world has ever seen.

DELIGHT

Why is Jesus's sacrifice on the cross for us so surprising from the world's perspective?

Paul says we are "dead" in our sin. In what ways does Jesus make us alive again?

DISPLAY

Since Jesus showed us incredible grace by dying for us, we should in turn show grace to others by how we treat them. Remember, grace is undeserved favor. Who in your life doesn't deserve your love? How can you show it to them anyway?

Dear God, thank You for making me alive in Christ. Thank You for giving me the grace that I could never earn or deserve. Help me to love others the way You love me. Help me to love You more and grow closer to You each day. Amen.

DAY 12

Don't Go Back!

READ ROMANS 6:15-23

For the wages of sin is death, but the gift of God is eternal life in Christ Jesus our Lord.
— Romans 6:23

DISCOVER

Darla, the child visiting the dentist's office in ***Finding Nemo***, is one of the funniest characters in Pixar history. Why is she shaking those poor fish? I don't blame Nemo for wanting to get back to the open water. Of course, he wanted to get back to his dad, but I would guess that freedom is better than the captivity of a fish tank and way better than a plastic bag!

When Jesus died on the cross, He took the punishment for the sins of everyone who believes in Him. This means that He takes care of all our sins—past, present, and future. In Romans 6, Paul asks an interesting question: Since we have grace and forgiveness for our sins, should we keep on freely sinning, knowing it is already forgiven? Paul emphatically answers no!

Sin is a death trap, and even though we are already forgiven and saved from eternal death, sin still has earthly consequences. Sin can destroy our relationships, peace, goals, and dreams, and it can lead us down paths we never want to take. Paul reminds us that we know what true freedom looks like. Going back and submitting ourselves to sin would be like putting on the chains of slavery again. It doesn't make any sense! It would be like Nemo finding his dad, then going back to live in Darla's plastic bag again! Jesus has freed us to follow Him and to live in the fullness of the life He brings. We cannot return to sin and the death that it brings.

DELIGHT

According to Paul, why should we not return to lives of sin?

Have you ever known someone who was freed from something but chose to return to it? What reasons did they have for slipping back into their old patterns?

What does this tell you about the danger of sin?

DISPLAY

What damage has your sin done in your life? Find the largest cup you have in your house. Then find the smallest measuring cup or spoon you have. Set them side by side. Living in sin after Jesus has freed you is like being extremely thirsty and drinking out of the small receptacle. Why would you do that when you have a larger cup you can use? Jesus freed us so we can walk in the fullness of life and escape the confines of our sin. Remember this example the next time you are tempted to choose the lesser way of sin.

Dear God, help me to live a full life by rejecting sin and accepting Your way of life. Thank You for the gifts of freedom and eternal life. Thank You for Your love, Your grace, and Your forgiveness. I love You, God. Help me to love You more deeply. Amen.

DAY 13

Grace in My Tank

READ 1 JOHN 1:5-9.

If we confess our sins, he is faithful and righteous to forgive us our sins and to cleanse us from all unrighteousness.
— 1 John 1:9

DISCOVER

Grace is best shown through what Jesus did for us on the cross, as we have seen over the past few days. It would be enough if grace only gave us salvation, but it's more than that. Grace is also what helps us to combat sin and live freely each day.

We know that even as Christians, we will have to battle against sin in our lives. That is why we need God's grace continually. Think about a car. It has all the tools it needs to drive all around town, carrying people where they need to go. But it needs gas to run, and you have to fill it up consistently so that it has the power to keep running. We need grace each day to live the life Jesus has made possible for us.

How do we receive grace? We can only receive grace by continually remembering what God has done for us through Jesus. In the book of 1 John, John reminds us that we must acknowledge our sins and bring them to God. If we claim to be without sin, we deny the gospel and deceive ourselves. The core of the good news of Jesus is that we are sinners who can only be cleansed of our sin through Jesus. Therefore, if we deny that we sin, we are essentially saying that we don't need Him. Instead, we confess our sins to God and rest in the knowledge that He will forgive us.

When we remember the power of the gospel and walk in the light of the truth, we receive grace. This grace is what we need to keep running through the highs and the lows of everyday life.

DELIGHT

Who or what do you rely on when you go through difficult times in life?

How does the gospel encourage us each day? Write down as many different encouragements as you can think of.

DISPLAY

Lamentations 3:22-23 reminds us that God's mercies are new every day. God has an unlimited amount of forgiveness and favor for you. Write the words "Unlimited Grace" on a sticky note and put the note on your bathroom mirror or inside your bedroom door. Sometimes, we can't recognize the grace God is giving us because we don't give ourselves any. Remember to forgive yourself, just as God has forgiven you through Jesus.

Dear Lord, thank You for another day. That is a gift from You to me. Thank You for Your grace for me. Help me to remember what You did for me through Jesus. Help me to extend grace to myself and those around me. Thank You for loving me even before I loved and knew You. Amen.

DAY 14

A Hard Gift to Accept

READ EPHESIANS 2:1-10.

For you are saved by grace through faith, and this is not from yourselves; it is God's gift — not from works, so that no one can boast.
— Ephesians 2:8-9

DISCOVER

Have you ever met a person who cannot accept a compliment? I struggle with this from time to time. If you try to praise me for something I do, I try to rationalize the compliment or deflect it toward someone else. I would like to believe it's humility, but it's really not. It's actually a pride problem (but that's another topic for another time). Even though compliments can be hard gifts to accept, we should welcome and be grateful for them. There is nothing wrong with accepting a compliment for hard work done. Don't worry—I'm working on it in my life!

Just as it's hard for me to simply accept a compliment, it's also sometimes hard for me to truly accept the gospel and rest in God's grace. Remember, Jesus's death in our place was an act of grace. We could never earn it, and we don't deserve it. But that doesn't stop us from trying. We serve God in our church out of obligation instead of grace overflowing in us. We watch what we do and say in public because we're putting on a show. We try to hide that we know we don't deserve grace. It would be best for us (and for those around us) if we admitted we were imperfect and joyfully accepted God's favor, even though we don't deserve it. To do so would bring us peace and rest and bring glory to God.

DELIGHT

Do you find yourself resting in God's grace or trying to earn it? If so how? If not, why?

What is so dangerous about feeling like you have to earn God's grace and forgiveness?

DISPLAY

You have to work for almost everything in life. That's what makes God's gift of grace so hard to accept. It's just about the only thing that you don't have to earn. Thankfully, you can grow in this area. Giving to others helps you become a better receiver of gifts. Make sure you practice giving: back to the Lord through a tithe, to others in love, and any time you feel like giving. And don't forget the compliments!

Dear Lord, thank You for Your loving-kindness. You don't have to care for me, but You do. Thank You for providing what I could never earn. Help me to rest in Your grace each day. Amen.

DAY 15

You Raise Me Up

READ JAMES 4.

Humble yourselves before the Lord, and he will exalt you.
— James 4:10

DISCOVER

Everyone needs a lift from time to time. Sometimes it's a stressful week that gets the best of us. Maybe life isn't going exactly the way you want it to. Perhaps it seems like you're taking more losses than wins. It happens to everyone, but that doesn't exactly make it feel better.

What can lift us up and make each day feel better? God's grace. We have already seen that we receive grace through confession and repentance. James tells us another pathway to grace: through practicing humility. Now, James doesn't want us to think poorly of ourselves. But he does want us to look at ourselves accurately in comparison to God. In fact, we can receive grace simply by thinking of ourselves less and focusing on God more. This goes hand in hand with what we know about the gospel. Remember, Jesus rescued us from a pit that we could never escape on our own. It's all about Him. When we are humble, we acknowledge that truth. It's all about God; it's all about Jesus. They are the reason we are where we are—it's only because of Jesus that we even have life.

How does this lift us up? God gives greater grace when we recognize Him as the ruler of our lives. We don't brag about our own accomplishments or talents; we submit to Him and give Him the glory for everything we have and all that we are. In turn, His power comes into us. It will be a huge boost to know that God is God and that He is in control. God's got you, so draw near to Him and rejoice in the arms of the King!

DELIGHT

How can you intentionally lean into God and tune out the world this week? Write down a few action steps below.

What in your life currently has you down? How does God's favor for you change your perspective in that area?

DISPLAY

One way you can think about grace is by remembering the acronym GRACE: *God's Riches At Christ's Expense*. Because of Jesus's sacrifice, God can freely give you good things: a relationship with Him, favor, forgiveness, love, joy, and peace. The list is endless—and it's because of what Jesus has done for you. The more we focus on Him, the more power and encouragement we will receive. Write this acronym somewhere special, or even design your own. Use it to remind you that every good thing you have is a result of God's grace and it came to you because of the price Jesus paid.

God, You are good. Thank You for remaining faithful despite my disobedience. Thank You for being good in my place. And thank You for being good to me. Amen.

DAY 16

Someone in Your Corner

READ HEBREWS 4:14-16.

Therefore, let us approach the throne of grace with boldness, so that we may receive mercy and find grace to help us in time of need.
— Hebrews 4:16

DISCOVER

In boxing, a cornerman (also knows as a second) is a trainer who comes to the boxer's aide in between rounds, offering advice, tips, and ice to help the boxer recover and continue to compete in the next round. Although life can throw punches at us, it's unlikely you need a real-life second at your disposal. For the believer, we have something infinitely better.

Hebrews 4 reminds us that Jesus is the ultimate cornerman. He is our High Priest in heaven. In the Old Testament, the high priest was the only person who could enter the innermost area of the temple, where the presence of God resided. It was the high priest's job to be a representative of the people and cry out to God for them.

The author of Hebrews is making clear that Jesus does that for us now. After Jesus was resurrected and rose into heaven, He took His rightful place at God's right hand. Since then, He has been interceding for us—that is, He has been talking to God on our behalf. Jesus constantly reminds God that He has died for us. Because of that sacrifice, we receive mercy: Jesus has taken the punishment for us. Who better to represent us? Jesus lived as a human and knows what we go through. It isn't that God needs reminding about what Jesus has done. It's for our benefit that we have a perfect High Priest who sympathizes with us and provides us with mercy and grace when we need it. When life beats us up, Jesus is there to help us stand—and win.

DELIGHT

We can bring our requests directly to God, through prayer. However, why is it comforting to you that Jesus is also making requests to God for us?

Jesus is unique in that He is one hundred percent God and also one hundred percent human. How does this reality make our relationship with God more personal? More relatable? More authentic?

DISPLAY

Read Exodus 29. In this chapter, God sets the rules for sacrifice as well as the preparation the priests need to make to enter His presence. We no longer offer sacrifices to make up for our sins because Jesus made the ultimate sacrifice for us. Now we have direct access to God because Jesus made it possible. Jesus is both the sacrifice and the High Priest. How does your view of Jesus change after you read Exodus 29?

Dear God, thank You for sending us Your Son, Jesus. Thank You for making a way for us to know You. Thank You for providing the ultimate High Priest for us, who takes away our sin and represents us before You. Thank You for hearing me when I pray. Amen.

MEMORY VERSES

For all have sinned
and fall short of the
glory of God; they
are justified freely
by his grace through
the redemption that
is in Christ Jesus.

— *Romans 3:23–24*

DAY 17

Bad News First

READ ROMANS 3:9-26.

For all have sinned and fall short of the glory of God; they are justified freely by his grace through the redemption that is in Christ Jesus.
— Romans 3:23-24

DISCOVER

Have you ever had news to tell someone, and that news had both good and bad parts to it? Did you ask them the famous question, "Do you want the good news or bad news first?" I always want the negativity first. At least then, the clouds will have a silver lining.

In Romans 3, Paul doesn't ask: he simply gives us the bad news first. This should be fine with us because the good news infinitely outweighs the bad. As we have already seen, everyone sins and falls short of God's perfection. Our sin deserves separation from God, and ultimately, death. That's the bad part. But the good news is this: we can be freely forgiven and made right with God because of Jesus. This is what it means to be justified: not only are we forgiven of our sins, but we are brought into a restored relationship with God. Jesus's perfection (that is, His righteousness) becomes yours. When you trust Jesus as Savior and Lord, you become a daughter or son of the King.

It's a bit like this: Imagine you were kicked off of a flight on the way to the beach. Being justified means that not only are you brought back onto the plane, but someone upgraded you to first class! Yes, we mess up, but Jesus makes it right, plus more. That's the power of grace!

DELIGHT

What has grace changed about your life?

Why is the good news of Jesus so much greater than the bad news of our sin?

Have you trusted Jesus as your Savior and Lord? Why or why not?

DISPLAY

If you haven't yet trusted Jesus as your Savior and Lord, talk to your pastor or another trusted adult. If you have, write your testimony in the space below. Your testimony is your story about how you heard about Jesus and put your faith in Him. Write down what your life was like before you met Jesus, what it was like when you put your faith in Him, and what He is teaching you now (or what He has most changed about your life).

Dear God, thank You for the good news of the gospel. You saw us in our sin, but You did not leave us there. You gave up Your only Son so that we could be Your children. Thank You for that incredible blessing. I love You, God. Amen.

DAY 18

Worth the Wait

READ 2 PETER 3:8-13.

The Lord does not delay his promise, as some understand delay, but is patient with you, not wanting any to perish but all to come to repentance.
— 2 Peter 3:9

DISCOVER

Amazon has revolutionized the way we shop. I still remember the days when I had to physically visit a store to purchase something I wanted or wait for my order to arrive in five to ten business days (excluding weekends!). However, now with Amazon, we can order almost anything and expect it to arrive at our doorstep the very next day. No more waiting!

Throughout history, every generation has pondered when Jesus will return. In 2 Peter, we learn that Jesus hasn't returned yet not because He's caught in traffic or taking a nap, but because He is patiently waiting for people to repent and turn to Him for salvation. He is waiting because of His grace. God doesn't want anyone to die without knowing Him—He desires a relationship with everyone.

For us, this means two things. First, we don't have to panic when we see the chaos of the world around us. God has everything in His plan and under control. Second, we need to share the gospel with others as we eagerly prepare for Jesus's arrival. We can help others experience the same grace that has transformed our lives. Until Jesus returns, we trust and serve Him. I assure you it will be worth the wait.

DELIGHT

What is one thing you cannot stand waiting for? Why?

Are you eager for Jesus to return? Why or why not?

What are you doing while you are waiting for Jesus to come back?

DISPLAY

In the last devotion, you wrote out your testimony. Have you ever shared your testimony with anyone? A great way to share the gospel with others is by sharing what Jesus has done in your life. Make a plan to share your testimony with someone this week, even a member of your family or another believer. Practice sharing until you are comfortable, and be prepared for God to give you an opportunity to share your story with someone who doesn't know Jesus yet.

Dear God, thank You for rescuing me from sin. Thank You for being patient with me and allowing me to turn to You. Thank You for being patient with others as well. Help me to be excited about Your return. Help me to be ready to share my story with others so they can meet You too. Amen.

DAY 19

Good Fruit

READ GALATIANS 5:16-26.

But the fruit of the Spirit is love, joy, peace, patience, kindness, goodness, faithfulness, gentleness, and self-control. The law is not against such things.
— Galatians 5:22-23

DISCOVER

It's important to keep in mind that small temptations can grow into evil desires, leading to sin and ultimately death. However, God's grace is also like a seed, and His fruit is much better. God's way is the best and most powerful, and His grace can lead to unbelievable results in our lives.

To receive grace, we need to remind ourselves of what Jesus did for us on the cross, confess our sins with true repentance, rest in grace instead of working for it, look to Jesus as our High Priest, and live humbly. Once we live powered by grace, we will walk in line with the Holy Spirit. Although the Holy Spirit lives in every believer, we need to submit to His leadership and listen to His voice. Grace helps us do this.

When we walk in step with the Holy Spirit, He produces fruit in our lives. Paul lists this fruit in Galatians 5:22-23. God desires for us to have all these things and live our lives characterized by them. With grace, we can achieve the fullness of life, which is beyond our imagination. While temptation leads to death, grace gives rise to a life of abundance. Grace is a powerful thing—praise God that He gives it to us!

DELIGHT

Where is your fruit of the Spirit lacking? Which area are you struggling with the most?

Which seed are you watering: the seed of temptation or the seed of grace? Explain.

DISPLAY

The fruit of the Spirit is the result of walking obediently with God throughout out lives. God wants us to produce all of the fruit of the Spirit, not just the parts that come more naturally. Thankfully, God will help us. Commit to praying specifically over the next week for the areas of the fruit of the Spirit that are harder for you. God wants to grow you in these areas so that your life will be full.

I love You, God. Thank You for providing me with the power to live a godly and full life. Show me where my weak spots are. Help me to grow in those areas today. Please give me opportunities to show the world Your glory. Amen.

DAY 20

Making a Difference

READ ROMANS 5:15-21.

If by the one man's trespass, death reigned through that one man, how much more will those who receive the overflow of grace and the gift of righteousness reign in life through the one man, Jesus Christ.
— Romans 5:17

DISCOVER

One person can make a huge difference. If we look at American History, we can think of a few names of people who have had a significant impact on our lives: leaders such as George Washington, activists like Martin Luther King, Jr. and Susan B. Anthony, and even amazing creators like Walt Disney.

In Romans 5, Paul compares two men who changed the entire course of creation. Adam, the first man, changed the world because of his sin, causing destruction and chaos to touch the earth and everything in it. But we can't be too hard on Adam, because we would have done the same thing if we were in his shoes. Every time we choose to do things our way, we are just like Adam.

Sin entered the world through one man, but it was also defeated by one man: Jesus Christ. Because of what Jesus has done, unlimited grace is available to us. It's an overflow: there is more than enough. Sometimes our sin seems insurmountable, but our wrong actions—even when we are at our worst—are no match for the wave of grace that Jesus can and wants to give us. That means no sin is too great to be forgiven. No mistake is too large to be redeemed. No stain is too big to be removed. His grace is greater than all of our sin.

DELIGHT

Have you ever felt like your sins and struggles were unforgivable? When? What were or are your struggles?

What truth from God's Word do you use to combat the lie that God's grace is not enough? What Scripture can remind you of the truth of God's grace?

DISPLAY

Take a moment to reflect on your answer to the first question on page 72. Ask if you are being honest with yourself, and identify any areas in your life where you feel unforgivable, isolated, or alone. Are you struggling with something that you haven't shared with God or others?

Search for a video of waves crashing on a beach. Observe how nothing can stop the waves from arriving on the beach time after time. If you allow Jesus and follow the steps we've discussed in this book, God's grace will be like those waves in your life. No sin or mistake will stand in the way of the favor and forgiveness that God wants to offer you.

Dear God, thank You for Your greatness. Our sin was immovable for us, yet You did what we couldn't do. Thank You for Your grace in my life. Help me to believe I am forgiven. Please help me to know that Your grace is enough. Amen.

SECTION 3
SHAMELESS

In the final section of this book, we'll explore how God erases our shame. This doesn't mean we can live thoughtlessly and do whatever we want. It means that because of God's grace, we can live beyond our shame and live in obedience to Him.

DAY 21

Freedom from Shame

READ ROMANS 6:1-14.

What should we say then? Should we continue in sin so that grace may multiply? Absolutely not! How can we who died to sin still live in it?
— Romans 6:1-2

DISCOVER

As a former sports writer, I once had the opportunity to interview a member of the Basketball Hall of Fame, and I remember how anxious I felt. I wanted to appear professional and worthy of the meeting, so I meticulously prepared myself by cleaning up, straightening my tie, and polishing my shoes. I made sure that everything was in place to avoid feeling unworthy.

Satan often attacks us through shame. Shame is a negative feeling that arises when we've done something wrong and feel guilty about our actions. God doesn't want us to live in shame; Jesus's sacrifice on our behalf has freed us from guilt for our sins. We are made righteous by God's grace, and therefore, we belong in His kingdom. Although shame tells us that we don't belong, God has restored us and says we are worthy.

To fight against shame, we must remain obedient to God and walk in freedom from sin. In other words, we won't feel shame when we don't live in sin. Although it's impossible to avoid sin altogether, we can ensure that we don't continue in old sinful patterns. Grace is a reminder that God's way is best, not an invitation to do as we please. We must reject old temptations and live obediently. Otherwise, we open the door to the enemy to bombard us with shame.

DELIGHT

When was a time you felt ashamed because of something you had done? How did you overcome that shame?

Jesus endured the ultimate shame. He was publicly ridiculed, physically abused, and put to death. He took upon Himself the sins of the world, and ultimately, became sin for us. All of this for you and for me. How does this reminder of the gospel aid you in fighting sin and shame in your life?

DISPLAY

Whenever you make your next sinful mistake, remind yourself of God's grace. Immediately pray to God and confess your sin. Ask Him to help you repent. Take responsibility for your sin and thank Jesus for taking your shame. Ask Him for more grace. When this happens, come back to this devotional and write in the blank below.

Did your immediate ownership, confession, and repentance help you in your fight against shame? Why or why not?

God, help me to walk away from the shame the enemy places on me. Help me to bask in Your forgiveness. Help me to put my sin to death. Thank You for Jesus's death, which means I am alive. Amen.

DAY 22

The Verdict

READ ROMANS 8:1-12.

Therefore, there is now no condemnation for those in Christ Jesus, because the law of the Spirit of life in Christ Jesus has set you free from the law of sin and death.
— Romans 8:1-2

DISCOVER

Maya Moore was a top WBNA basketball player until she found another way to use her talents and voice to impact the world. During her team's community outreach, she met a man named Jonathan Irons, who she believed was wrongfully convicted of a burglary crime. He was serving a fifty-year sentence in prison, which would take most of his life. Maya stopped her career and worked endlessly to help overturn that conviction. Jonathan was released in 2020. He was truly innocent, and "not guilty" must have been two of the best words he had ever heard.

As humans, all of us are guilty of sin, as we have already seen in this devotional. We are guilty, but because of grace, we will hear the words "not guilty" when we arrive at God's throne. We are not condemned (judged for our wrongdoing) because Jesus has already taken our punishment for us.

Since God doesn't see us as guilty, we don't have to be ashamed. We are forgiven and free. We don't have to feel ashamed of our past. We don't have to wallow in shame because of our struggles. We are no longer sentenced to death; our conviction has been overturned. Remind yourself constantly of that truth: because of Jesus, you are declared not guilty.

DELIGHT

How do you think Jonathan Irons felt when he heard the words "not guilty"? List as many emotions as you can think of that he might have felt.

Do you feel those emotions when you think about what Jesus did for you? Why or why not?

DISPLAY

Because of Jesus, we are no longer condemned or declared guilty. Instead, God's Word guides us into what is best. However, the pain of our sin can still hurt. This is why God wants to use His grace to set us free. When we realize what He has done, we will obey: not because we are afraid of the consequences, but because we love our Savior dearly. What rules do you find hardest to follow? Why do you believe God has given us those particular rules? What is your motivation for obeying God?

God, help me to obey You because I love You. I know I am free because of Your grace. Help me to follow what is best for me. Thank You for declaring me "not guilty" even though I mess up. Thank You for sending me Jesus, who was perfect for me. I love You, God. Amen.

DAY 23

You Belong with Me

READ ROMANS 10:1-13.

There is no distinction between Jew and Greek,
because the same Lord of all richly blesses all who call on him.
— Romans 10:12

DISCOVER

A sense of belonging can be very helpful in overcoming shame. Shame is a feeling that arises from wrongdoing, but it's also partially caused by fear. We feel shame when we believe that others know about our mistakes. We can be more afraid of what others think (our perception) than what is actually true (the reality). However, when we feel accepted and loved, it wipes away shame because this is a more powerful feeling that speaks to the heart of who we are.

Our soul desires to belong to God's family, but sin separates us from Him. To have a relationship with God, sin had to be defeated. That victory was achieved for us, and we share in the victory through faith in Jesus. Jesus was subjected to the most humiliating death in the history of the world. The Son of God was crucified for crimes He didn't commit. He was oppressed and tormented, but He did not open his mouth to speak in His own defense. He was put to shame, but He was not ashamed of you.

This is the key to escaping shame in your life. When you see what Jesus did for you—that He loves you so much that He was willing to die in your place—it changes your perspective. You take Jesus more seriously than you take yourself. What people think about you becomes less important because what Jesus says about you is unchanging: He says that no matter your mistakes, He loves you. Through Jesus's death, He has proved that He wants you.

DELIGHT

What is an important group for you to belong to? Why is it important to you?

When have you been afraid of what others think of you?

What does it tell you about God that despite your mistakes, He is not ashamed of you?

DISPLAY

Get a sheet of paper and draw a line down the middle. On one side, write down things that other people have said about you. On the other side of the paper, write down what God says about you. Feel free to use your Bible or a resource online for help. Which side contains the more powerful statements? Which side do you tend to believe the most?

Dear God, thank You for the truth that You have spoken of over me. Help me to believe it every day of my life. Thank You that I belong with You forever. Amen.

DAY 24

Cease and Resist

READ 1 CORINTHIANS 10:1-13.

No temptation has come upon you except what is common to humanity. But God is faithful; he will not allow you to be tempted beyond what you are able, but with the temptation he will also provide the way out so that you may be able to bear it.
— 1 Corinthians 10:13

DISCOVER

Healthy eating can be challenging, especially when there's an excellent cook in your household. Imagine a day of successfully eating well and then coming home and seeing a plate of warm, gooey cinnamon rolls waiting on the stove. It would be tough to resist the temptation!

In the last devotion, we learned how belonging can help us overcome shame. Learning how to fight against temptation is another tool in our arsenal to defeat shame. Satan is well-versed in attacking us. He knows what we think and what we desire. However, God has promised that there is a way out of temptation, and through it, we can emerge victorious.

In 1 Corinthians 10, Paul reminds us about how God's people, the Israelites, failed to obey Him in various areas, particularly in idolatry. Their primary sin was replacing God with other things in their lives. We make that mistake as well. When we are tempted by our idols, we normally fall to them. The escape from temptation lies in keeping God first in our lives. When we desire God more than anything else, we will not fall into temptation. When we choose to love God over everything else (even over the cinnamon rolls) we can obey Him and resist sin. Keep God first and temptation loses its power.

DELIGHT

Do you normally learn from your mistakes? Do you learn well from the mistakes of others? Why or why not?

What in your life have you been tempted to place ahead of God?

DISPLAY

Revisit Day 4 of this devotional. In that activity, you wrote down areas of temptation and asked for accountability from someone you know. Now, it's time to evaluate. How is that area of struggle currently going? Have you been updating your accountability partner? Have you been successful in fighting against that temptation? What steps do you now need to take to fight it or continue to succeed against it?

Dear God, thank You for giving me the power to stand strong against temptation. Help me to never let sin become normal in my life—help me to battle against it every day. Help me to keep You as the most important thing in my life. Amen.

DAY 25

Stepping In

READ HEBREWS 12:1-12.

Therefore, since we also have such a large cloud of witnesses surrounding us, let us lay aside every hindrance and the sin that so easily ensnares us. Let us run with endurance the race that lies before us, keeping our eyes on Jesus, the pioneer and perfecter of our faith. For the joy that lay before him, he endured the cross, despising the shame, and sat down at the right hand of the throne of God.
— Hebrews 12:1-2

DISCOVER

Have you ever made a mistake and had someone else take the blame for you? We know it's wrong, but it's a relief when someone else assumes responsibility for our actions, even if it wasn't their fault. This is what Jesus did for us when He took our shame upon Himself and went through extreme humiliation on the cross. He was shamed so we wouldn't have to be.

On the cross, we also see another way in which Jesus defeated shame. Jesus decided that we were worth going through that horrific ordeal. As a result, He received us, which brought Him joy! He was also lifted up, glorified, and seated at the right hand of God. Though His shame was great, His reward was infinitely greater. The same is true for us. If we can get past our shame, the result will be worth it.

For us, what lies beyond shame? Victory, closeness with God, and honor. Jesus paved the way through shame so that we can follow behind Him. Remember, Jesus died so that the battle against sin and death would be won for all eternity. Shame tries to steal the victory that has already been won. It suggests that Jesus's work is not enough for us. When we can get past these lies, we realize that the pain of shame was nothing compared to the experience of victory and the joy of God's presence.

DELIGHT

Have you ever thought about how difficult Jesus's death was, even for Him? How does this make you feel?

How does the reality of the crucifixion change how you see the difficult parts of your life?

Describe a moment of shame you recently experienced. How did you get past it?

DISPLAY

Who are you most following in your life right now? If it isn't Jesus, you're not following the best. When we don't follow the best leaders, that leads to mistakes. Shame threatens to creep in. What characteristics of Jesus's life do you need to follow right now? What lessons from Jesus's death do you need to apply to your life right now?

Dear God, thank You for Jesus's example in my life. Thank You for sending Him to step in and take my place in perfection and death. Help me to triumph over shame so that I can grow closer to You. Thank You for Jesus's endurance. Help me to keep pressing forward, too. Amen.

DAY 26

A Special Delivery

READ ROMANS 1:16-32.

For I am not ashamed of the gospel, because it is the power of God for salvation to everyone who believes, first to the Jew, and also to the Greek.
— Romans 1:16

DISCOVER

I love Christmas! It's the time of the year when we focus on the amazing story of Jesus being delivered to us. For my family, it's also a time to prioritize giving gifts to one another. Imagine receiving a shirt for Christmas that you really wanted. Would you be ashamed to show it off to other people or would you wear it with pride? You'd wear it every chance you got!

Similarly, we shouldn't be ashamed of the gospel, the good news about Jesus's death in our place. It is the only way to God and the power to receive eternal life. Sin brings us shame, but Jesus brings us life and joy. We cannot be ashamed of how we received forgiveness because on our own, we would have only received death.

In Romans 1, Paul explains that God allows those who reject Jesus to live in their sin and even fall deeper into it. Only when we realize the destruction that sin causes will we recognize our need for a Savior. When people reject Jesus, they reject the only way to salvation. No one can escape the grasp of sin on his or her own.

That's what makes Jesus's sacrifice so amazing. Even while you and I were His enemies, He died for us. As believers, we must reveal Jesus wherever we go, hoping that others will see the power of God in us and accept that personally for themselves. As we have been delivered from shame, we must champion our Savior so that others can experience the same.

DELIGHT

Is salvation the greatest gift you have received? If so, do you treat it like it is? If not, what could possibly be a greater gift?

Salvation is a gift you can share with others. When was the last time you had a conversation about Jesus with someone? Is there something holding you back from having your next one? If so, what?

DISPLAY

Find a gift box or gift bag. Prepare it as if you were giving a gift to the most important person in your life. On the outside, label it "Salvation" and place it somewhere you will see it. Use this gift to remind yourself that if you had nothing else, salvation is what you really need. It's the greatest gift ever given.

Dear God, thank You for being a giving God. You have everything and yet You don't keep it to Yourself. You give to us even when we don't deserve it. Thank You for Your faithfulness and that You didn't let our sin stop You from Your love. Help me to see the depth of Your love for me. Amen.

MEMORY VERSES

*Therefore, there is now no
condemnation for those
in Christ Jesus, because the
law of the Spirit of life in
Christ Jesus has set you
free from the law of sin
and death.*

— Romans 8:1–2

DAY 27

Get Your Shine On

READ PSALM 34.

Those who look to him are radiant with joy;
their faces will never be ashamed.
— Psalm 34:5

DISCOVER

Making a wise decision is never something you'll regret. Even if it's unpopular or people ridicule you or look down on you, it will always be beneficial to your life. It's what God wants. The Bible tells us that "fear of the LORD is the beginning of wisdom" (Prov. 9:10), so choosing God's way will always be the right choice.

In Psalm 34, David said that those who look to the Lord will never be put to shame. Even when others look down on you, God won't. Eternally, that is the only thing that matters. And the more we see things God's way, the more it won't matter when people judge us on earth, either. We must look to God and obey Him. When we do, it will pay off. While you may experience temporary embarrassment or shame when you return to sinful ways, if you look to Jesus as your Lord and Savior, you're freed from that shame. Jesus has already taken your sin and paid for it on the cross.

Because we're free from shame, we can confidently enter God's presence and receive His grace and love. When we rest in Him, there is no shame. The more we rely on Him, the greater we will shine. We'll receive joy, and we'll be reminded that nothing can separate us from Him. This truth will carry us through the toughest times and give us hope.

DELIGHT

What does it mean to look to God?

How do you enter His presence? Do you make time with God a regular rhythm of your life?

Have you felt the joy of God smiling down on you? Why or why not?

DISPLAY

If you are in Christ, when God looks at you, He sees the perfection of Jesus. So, the real question is: Are you looking to Him? Looking to God includes reading and following His Word, worshiping Him in song and with your obedience, and resting in His presence in prayer and meditation. If you aren't regularly practicing these disciplines, ask your pastor or a trusted adult for help. The more you look to God, the more you will shine. God's joy is a glow that is hard for anyone to wipe off.

Dear God, thank You for smiling down upon me. Help me to spend consistent time in Your presence so I can receive Your joy. Thank You for never putting me to shame and for freeing me from its weight. I love You, God. Amen.

DAY 28

Better to Give

READ MARK 8:34-38.

Calling the crowd along with his disciples,
he said to them, "If anyone wants to follow after me,
let him deny himself, take up his cross, and follow me."
— Mark 8:34

DISCOVER

When we prioritize the needs of others over our own, it brings a sense of fulfillment. It's fascinating how serving others, donating our resources without any self-serving motives, or helping someone in her or his time of need can uplift not only this person's day but our own life as well.

It required an incredible act of humility for Jesus to sacrifice Himself for us. The same path to overcoming shame in our lives is through humility. Humility isn't thinking less of ourselves—it's thinking highly of Jesus. To be humble, we must simply think of ourselves less. Jesus was the most exceptional servant the world has ever seen. He was the only One who truly deserved ultimate glory, yet He put it aside for us.

In Mark 4, Jesus says that we should deny ourselves, which means we must reject our own desires and submit ourselves to what God wants. It means that we don't prioritize ourselves on our wish lists; instead, we consider others as more important than ourselves. This mentality is "others first." Jesus's way overcomes shame because there is nothing shameful about focusing on others. By disregarding our selfish desires and putting our old sinful ways to death, we overcome shame. Giving feels good, not because we are congratulating ourselves, but because we are following the way of Jesus. When we follow His path, it goes well for us, too.

DELIGHT

Do you think the people around you would describe you as a humble person? Why or why not?

What selfish desire do you need to let God destroy?

What is a practical way you can put others first this week?

DISPLAY

One of the markers of selfishness is making complaints. According to a study, the average person complains around fifteen to thirty times per day. It's unhealthy, and at its core, it's selfish. Tomorrow, see how many times you complain. After you track your complaints for a few days, you'll be more aware of any selfish tendencies you have. From there, you can ask God to help you be more "other focused" and begin to grow in humility.

Dear God, help me to be more like Your Son, Jesus. Help me to be humble and place others above myself. I know I can only do this through Your power, so please continue to work in my life. Help me to be characterized by thanksgiving, not complaining. I love You, God. Amen.

DAY 29

It's Just Temporary

READ 1 PETER 5:6-11.

The God of all grace, who called you to his eternal glory in Christ, will himself restore, establish, strengthen, and support you after you have suffered a little while.
— 1 Peter 5:10

DISCOVER

For me, going to the dentist is like torture. No offense to any dentists out there, but I cannot stand the dentist's office. They make you hold your mouth at an awkwardly open position, place an alarming number of sharp metal objects in your mouth, and then try to have a conversation with you for an hour. The only way I make it through a trip to the dentist is that I know that it is a benefit to my overall health. I also know that the visit won't last forever. It won't be long before I escape the smells and can breathe fresh air once more.

Life can be difficult at times. In 1 Peter 5, Peter reminds us that we have an enemy who wants to separate us from God and entice us into disobedience. However, if we are in Christ, we cannot be separated from the love of Jesus. We can still be tempted, but two truths can encourage us. First, anything that we go through can bring us closer to God and make us stronger. Second, the battle with Satan will not last forever. Either way—whether Jesus comes back to get us or we die and leave this earth—we will be free of Satan's influence and able to live fully in the victory that Jesus has made possible for us.

Therefore, take a deep breath and remember that whatever you are going through is temporary. God is with you, and He will never leave you. On the other side of your battle with the enemy is more of God's grace waiting to lift you up once more.

DELIGHT

What is something difficult that you're going through right now?

Does it encourage you to know that your situation is temporary? Why or why not?

DISPLAY

Find a piece of rope or a thread. Lay it down horizontally on a flat surface, and make a mark close to the end of with a permanent marker. If your mark is on the right end of the rope, flip it around so that it is on the left-hand side. Did you know that your life is short compared to eternity? Your life is like the short distance of the rope before the mark, and eternity is after the mark. You haven't even reached your prime yet!

An eternal perspective eases the burden of our circumstances. One day, and for eternity, we will be in heaven with our Savior, away from any of sin's impact. Knowing that even the worst of times are temporary helps us persevere through them.

Dear God, thank You for another day. Even when things don't go my way, help me to see them as You see them. Help me to know that You are with me, even when I don't feel it. Thank You for promising to deliver me from evil, even if that won't be until I reach heaven. Thank You for Your promises, which never fail. Amen.

DAY 30

The Benediction

READ NUMBERS 6:22-27.

'"May the LORD bless you and protect you;
may the LORD make his face shine on you
and be gracious to you;
may the LORD look with favor on you
and give you peace."'
— Numbers 6:24-26

DISCOVER

Sometimes in a conversation, we tend to remember whatever the other person said last. My prayer for you is that you remember this devotion, especially this last word. In many churches, pastors end the service with a benediction—a prayer of blessing over the people until they meet again. In Numbers 6, God asks His priests to bless the people in this way. God wanted them to forget the lies of the enemy and remember how He really felt about them.

God already sees you as His beloved son or daughter. Because of what Jesus has done, you are a part of His family, and no one can change that. He wants to give you more grace than you could ever imagine. God has already given His Son for you—no gift could be greater than what He has already given.

So, how does this practically change our lives? When you look at your life, do you see things positively or negatively? Since God has gone to unimaginable lengths to bring us into a relationship with Him, why would He abandon us now? Since He wants to give us more grace, the difficult things in our lives must be for our good and not to harm us. Since He had a plan for us when we were His enemy in sin, He surely has a plan for us now after He has freed us from sin's grasp. When we remind ourselves of the truth, we will see things as God sees them. It all depends on how we look at it, with human eyes or with a heavenly perspective!

DELIGHT

How do you believe God feels about you? Do you believe He is disappointed with you, or do you believe He looks at you with unshakable love? Why?

What has the "favor of the Lord" recently looked like in your life?

DISPLAY

Let's talk about two habits I'd like you to try to make in your life as we end this devotional. One, make it a habit to look back on your life and thank the Lord for what He has done. Often, God is working and placing grace in our lives, but we are too busy to notice it. Stopping and thanking God will make us able to more clearly see His work. Two, do your best to bless others as God commands the priests to do in Numbers 6. To spread grace, we should speak life over others and see to it that we are not leading others in the opposite direction.

Dear God, thank You for smiling down upon me. I know I don't deserve it, but thank You for what Jesus made possible for me on the cross. Thank You for Your love and favor, and please help me to show that same love to others. I love You, God. Amen.

CAN I GET A RE-DO?

We all have moments that we probably wish we could forget. It might take years before we're finally able to laugh about these moments instead of cringing when someone brings them up. Regardless of how we feel about those embarrassing times, we all have them. So, let's do a quick countdown. Write out your five most embarrassing moments, with five being the least embarrassing and one being the most embarrassing.

5

4

3

2

1

Out of our embarrassing moments sometimes comes the wish for a time machine, for the ability to redo what's been done by us or to us.

A TAINTED VIEW

Sometimes shame hits us because of things beyond our control—the things we're embarrassed about but can't change, like our physical appearance, our family of origin, our social status, the sound of our voice, or the way we laugh.

Each of these things was originally intended to be beautiful and perfect. God designed people in His image, after all. He uniquely crafts each of our bodies, minds, and hearts. He knows our personalities and how He can use them for our good, the good of others, and His glory. He designed family to be a safe place, where people could be loved for who they are and kept safe from the dangers beyond their homes. He created us all to take care of each other so that none of those in need would go neglected.

But sin has tainted the world, and it no longer runs according to God's original design. So these ideals are often quite far from our reality.

That leaves us in a bit of a predicament. How do we learn to love the things about ourselves that sin has tainted, whether it's through the way we view them with our own eyes or the way we perceive them based on the words and actions of others?

Because of sin, we can be tempted to think that anything other than what we are is better. Let's look at some of the tainted views you have about things you can't change.

What are some qualities about your physical appearance you wish you could change? Where do you think this view of yourself came from? Why do you want to change those things?

Do you sometimes wish you could change your personality or the way you're perceived in the world? Why or why not?

When have you struggled to accept your family of origin? Why?

If you don't know where you're from, how has that affected the way you look at yourself?

OUR SHAME

Sometimes shame hits us because of something we've done that we know is wrong. Maybe you clearly understood the action as wrong before you did it, or maybe you just had a vague feeling of discomfort. Maybe you experienced a slight hesitation and asked yourself, "Is this really the best idea?" But then, you did it anyway. Or maybe you had no clue until the consequences unfolded fully. Lesson learned, right?

That's the thing about shame over sin: we can feel it, but we don't have to live in it because of Jesus. He took on our sin and our shame on the cross. When we know we've done wrong and repent (meaning we tell Him about it, ask for forgiveness, and turn away from that action or habit), we are immediately forgiven—even though we'll likely still face the consequences of our actions.

Imagine the worst thing you've ever done. On a scale of 1 to 10, how do you feel about that action now?

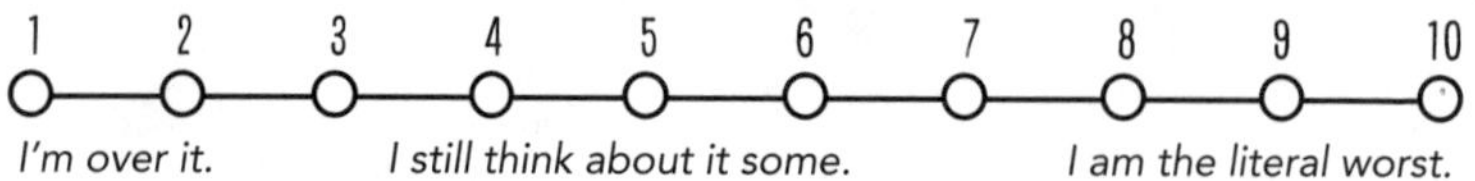

I'm over it. *I still think about it some.* *I am the literal worst.*

List two things that you've done that you're still ashamed of.

What were the consequences of these actions?

If you have repented of those things and sought the forgiveness of God—and, if possible, of the other people involved—then it's okay to let it go. You don't have to keep punishing yourself. When Jesus died, He took that punishment for you. There's no need for a do-over here. It's done. Over. Finished.

Why do you think it's hard letting go of the shame over some of the things you've done?

CHEAP SHOTS

Just like we might feel ashamed of things about ourselves that we can't change, that simply arise from living in a world wrecked by sin, we also might feel ashamed because of things that have been done to us.

These issues can be hard to talk about or even triggering, so if you need to skip this section or work through it with someone you trust, feel free. This is for you, and ultimately, it's between you and Jesus.

So, let's keep this simple, shall we? What has been done to you that you feel a sense of shame over?

A NEW VIEW

Now, take a few minutes to imagine what it would be like to live in a world where you feel no shame. Zero. Zip. Nada.

As you imagine, try to put it on paper or record it somehow. Write a poem or song, create a collage, paint, draw, journal, or even record a video of yourself talking about how you envision this world.

Did you know that world is coming? And in some ways, it's already here? While you might still feel the echoes of shame and the pain of the consequences of your wrongdoing, they don't rest on your shoulders when you turn to Jesus.

He says, "Come to me, all of you who are weary and burdened, and I will give you rest. Take my yoke upon you and learn from me, because I am lowly and humble in heart, and you will find rest for your souls. For my yoke is easy and my burden is light" (Matt. 11:28-30).

Jesus forgives you when you ask. He carries your burdens, eases the weight of your failures and shame, and gives you rest for each day. But one day, we will experience full and final rest with Him.

In His grace, God provided Jesus. In His grace, God made a way for us to be saved. In His grace, God made a way for us to be forgiven and live eternally in His presence, where there will be no more sin and no more shame. Everything will be as it was intended in the beginning. But for now, God calls us to come to Him with our sin, our sorrow, and our shame. He calls us to release those things to Him and trust in His grace to cover us. And, though it might feel impossible sometimes, He empowers us to extend that grace to those who've wronged us too.